A TIM MOONEY PUBLICATION

FIRST PUBLISHED 1999

ALL PHOTOGRAPHY: TIM MOONEY
FILM: KODAK, SYDNEY
PROCESSING: METRO PHOTO, ARTARMON, SYDNEY
HELICOPTER PILOTS: PAT SOURS, SCOTT BOWERS, PETER HOLSTEIN, MICHAEL LOBB

PRODUCTION: **DESIGN & STYLE**: FIONA COTTEE
REPRODUCTION & PRINTING: IMAGO SINGAPORE

Sydney WATERFRONTS

[By Tim Mooney]

THANKS

Particular thanks to the following organisations whose support made this volume possible.

COLLIERS JARDINE

AUSTRALIAN NATIVE LANDSCAPES
BMW SYDNEY
KODAK
ORACLE

ADDITIONAL THANKS

to Lynn, Ben and Amanda Mooney for their patience and support, Fiona Cottee for her masterful design touch and guidance, Kevin and Marjo Mooney for their hospitality, Mother and Father for making the sun shine, Bill Tregear, Russell Debney, Deborah Halla, Daphne Van Reekum, Bill Bradley for his endearing optimism, the team at Bradleys, Metro Photo for their outstanding service, Jim Bourke, Ross Penman, Peter Ratray, Garry Crowhurst, Barbara Ell, Margie Blok, Jonathan Chancellor, Pat Soars, Scott Bowers, Bruce Walker, Chris Mooney for the Web Design, Phil Kiely, John Harlen, John Parkinson, Nick and Tracey Clayton, Robert Kiyosaki for his wisdom and support over the years, and to everyone that helped.

Official Imaging
Partner of the 2000
Olympic Games

BMW Sydney

Sydney WATERFRONTS

[By Tim Mooney]

INTRODUCTION

Sydney cherishes its waterfrontage.
Despite the ever-inward residential sprawl, the spotlight has never really shifted far from the glittering water's edge. Socialites and socialists fight for space on Sydney's magnetic waterfront.
Their sunlit mansions mirrored along the expansive waterways, like expensive jewels in a turquoise Antipodean crown.
Little wonder almost all these waterfronts will command million dollar prices by early this twentyfirst century.
The coastal properties featured in Tim Mooney's book are the most prized residential possessions in Australia.
Carthona, the Colonial Regency-style residence on the shores of Darling Point, was built in 1841 to be seen and admired.
Just as enduring have been the sandstone mansions built by the Jeanneret and Joubert families along the Hunters Hill peninsula in the late 1800s.
The Spanish Mission-style, Boomerang, that touch of Hollywood on the harbour, at Elizabeth Bay, joined the dress circle of homes in 1925.
Contoured into the bushland Middle Harbour terrain were the Walter Burley Griffin homes during the 1920s and 1930s.
On the Pittwater, the futurist weekender, Kumale, was built in 1955, a hint of the importance of individualistic architecture yet to come.
Highrises really started towering the skyline, from Cronulla to Mona Vale, during the 1960s.
Starting on the Birchgrove peninsula, the redundant industrial waterfront workshops were turned into contemporary townhouse sites by astute entreprenuers in the 1980s.
As the 2000 Olympics neared, the trend hastened, heading all the way up the Lane Cove and Parramatta rivers.
Windfall profits from the 1990s sharemarket saw monolithic contemporary homes replace the bulldozed residences especially along the Balmoral and Point Piper waterfronts.

Bennelong, the controversial CBD apartment block, which stands adjacent to The Sydney Opera House, became the latest addition in mid-1999.
And if one doesn't own a waterfront, or live within cooee to enjoy the vista, the sheer plenitude of water, and egalitarian streak that runs deep in our psyche, ensures access for all.
Residents and tourists are invariably waterborne on powered boats, surfboards, yachts, dinghies, replica First Fleeters, and ferries. All giving Sydney waterways their colourful vitality.
The splendour from the air, however, has been reserved for an exclusive few – and windowseat passengers, arriving or departing from Kingsford Smith Airport, get fleeting views only.
Tim Mooney's book unlocks the aerial aspect of the coves within bays and bays within coves for all to enjoy.
His regular helicopter flights have ensured the waterfront stretches and the houses which line the ridges have been captured at their sparkling best.
The kaleidoscopic photographs are inspirational.
The book will not only add to the unrivalled esteem in which Sydney holds itself, but will unquestionably contribute to the ongoing tribal debate about which particular waterfront aspect beats them all.

JONATHAN CHANCELLOR
PROPERTY EDITOR
SYDNEY MORNING HERALD

Sydney WATERFRONTS

CONTENTS

northern
BEACHES

Arriving at Manly Cove, the Harbour's gateway to Sydney's very popular Northern Beaches

Looking south over Cabbage Tree Bay with Shelly Beach and Fairy Bower rock pool

THE LIFESTYLE AT FAIRY BOWER IS VERY RELAXED

Fairy Bower point at Shelly Beach Park is a very popular acquatic recreation destination

North Steyne Beach joining Manly Beach with Sydney Harbour in the back–

Freshwater Beach in the foreground with Manly beyond

SYDNEY WATERFRONTS · 19

Looking south over Dee Why Head to Curl Curl Beach

North Curl Curl

DEE WHY ABOVE, BELOW LEFT AND MIDDLE. BELOW RIGHT: SOUTH CURL CURL

Looking south over Long Reef Point, Long Reef Golf Course, Long Reef Beach and Dee Why Beach

Fishermans Beach, Collaroy Basin

COLLAROY BEACH, NARRABEEN BEACH WITH THE NARRABEEN LAKES IN THE BACKGROUND. BELOW LEFT AND RIGHT: COLLAROY BEACH

Left top to bottom: Narrabeen Head rock bath, Turimetta Beach, North Narrabeen. Main photo: Narrabeen to Collaroy.

Turimetta Head, Turimetta Beach, North Narrabeen Beach and Narrabeen Lakes

Above: Basin Beach.
Above Top: Mona Vale Beach
with Pittwater in the background.
Right: Looking North over
Warriewood Beach, Mona Vale
Beach and Basin Beach

Looking over Bungan Head to Bungan Beach

Above top: Bungan Beach
Above: Bungan Head Reserve
to Newport baths and beach
Right: Newport Beach with
Little Reef off Bungan Head

Full moon and moderate seas at Newport's sea pool

Above top: Bilgola Head
Above: Bilgola rock baths and beach
Right: Bilgola Beach

Summer at Bilgola Beach

*Above: Avalon Beach
and northern headland
'Hole in the Wall'
Above top:
St Michael's Cave through
to Bangalley Head
Left: South of Avalon
Beach, Bilgola Head with
Avalon Golf Course*

Avalon Beach

Below top left & right: Careel Head
Bottom left: Rock baths and beach
Bottom right & main photo:
North Whale Beach and Little Head

Whale Beach

LEFT: CABBAGE TREE BOAT HARBOUR AND SOUTH PALM BEACH.   BELOW: LITTLE HEAD WITH WHALE BEACH TO THE REAR, ABOVE: PALM BEACH.

Looking south over Barrenjoey Headland and Palm Beach with the Tasman Sea on the left and Pittwater on the right

Pittwater from the west with Scotland Island

Salt Pan Point

middle HARBOUR

Hunters Bay including Balmoral Beach, Rocky Point and Edwards Beach

Hunters Bay to the left
including Balmoral Beach,
Rocky Point and Edwards
Beach with Wy-ar-gine Point
in the foreground and
Chinamans Beach to the right.

Chinamans Beach

Above top: Wy-ar-gine Point
Above: Shell Cove
Right: The Spit through to the Heads

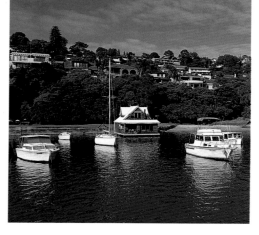

ABOVE LEFT: PEARL BAY, RIGHT: FOLLY POINT. BELOW LEFT: LONG BAY, RIGHT: QUAKERS HAT BAY, LONG BAY AND WILLOUGHBY BAY

Quakers Hat Bay, Mosman

Looking south over Beauty Point (lower left) through to the city

ABOVE: LEFT – NORTHBRIDGE AND SAILORS BAY, RIGHT – CASTLECRAG, BELOW: LEFT – SUGARLOAF POINT, RIGHT – CASTLECRAG AND SUGARLOAF BAY

ABOVE AND BELOW: SAILORS BAY, NORTHBRIDGE

Sugarloaf Point in the foreground through to The Heads

Tranquillity in Middle Harbour

Clontarf Beach

North Harbour with Fourty Baskets Beach

northern PORT JACKSON

Little Sirius Cove, Taronga Zoological Park, Athol Bay and Bradleys Head

Neutral Bay, Kurraba Point, Shell Cove, Cremorne Point, Mosman Bay, Curraghbeena Point and Little Sirius Cove

Cremorne Point

Kirribilli

Neutral Bay, Shell Cove

The view from Cremorne Point

eastern SUBURBS

ABOVE: SOUTH HEAD TO SHARK BAY, NIELSEN PARK AND STEEL POINT. BELOW: VAUCLUSE POINT TO VAUCLUSE BAY. RIGHT: VAUCLUSE BAY

ABOVE LEFT: PARSLEY BAY, ABOVE RIGHT: VILLAGE POINT, BELOW LEFT: CAMP COVE, LAINGS POINT AND WATSONS BAY. BELOW RIGHT: VAUCLUSE BAY

Above: Point Piper
Right: Rose Bay

Point Piper below top and right. Bottom left Woollahara Point jutting out into Rose Bay

High rise view from Woolsley Rd, Point Piper

ABOVE: DOUBLE BAY, BELOW: VARIOUS ACQUATIC ACTIVITY. OPPOSITE PAGE – TOP: DOUBLE BAY, BOTTOM: DARLING POINT

ABOVE: POINT PIPER, REDLEAF POOL, POINT PIPER. BELOW: DARLING POINT. OPPOSITE PAGE: DARLING POINT TO RUSHCUTTERS BAY

Rushcutters Bay and The Cruising Yacht Club of Australia– Sydney 2000 Olympics Sailing headquarters

The BMW Sydney Winter Series is the biggest sailing regatta in the Southern Hemisphere

SYDNEY HARBOUR – PORT JACKSON – IS A PERFECT NATURAL FACILITY FOR VARIED SAILING ACTIVITY

Oracle's "Sayonara" leads the fleet out of Sydney Harbour in the Sydney to Hobart Yacht Race.

*Above: Sayonara's crew
in fair weather
Opposite Page and right:
Sayonara and
Brindabella 'flying'
down the coast in the
1998 Sydney to Hobart
Blue Water Classic.*

high
LIVING

In recent years Sydney Harbour's most pronounced foreshore changes have resulted from the city's new found residential passion for high-rise harbour living. Sydney high-rise is a niche market and international real estate agency Colliers Jardine has sold a major share of apartments in landmark Sydney foreshore buildings during the past five years, dominating the marketplace. Attracting owner-occupiers to breathtaking views and investors to the potential of high capital growth, high-rise harbourfront developments have transformed commercial property areas such as Circular Quay, Milsons Point and Balmain into internationally renowned residential localities.

Many spectacular apartment buildings have been born from office building conversions such as Observatory Tower in East Circular Quay. The Peninsular apartments in East Balmain were redeveloped from the historic Colgate Palmolive factory. The recent development of No. 1 Macquarie Street, known as Bennelong and adjacent to the Opera House, is arguably Sydney's highest profile address. Colliers Jardine's residential project marketing team considers Bennelong unique, being the only property along nearly 14 kilometres of Sydney CBD waterfrontage that can be owned outright, rather than being subject to a '99 year lease to the Government.

The following high living section of 'Sydney Waterfronts' features some of Sydney's best known high-rise landmark apartment properties located along the city's harbour foreshores.

A new residence at 28 Billyard Ave, Elizabeth Bay has a magnificent Northerly aspect to the harbour

Elizabeth Bay

Woolloomooloo Bay

LEFT: WOOLLOOMOOLOO BAY. ABOVE: SWIM LEG IN THE WORLD CUP TRIATHALON HEAT ON THE OLYMPIC COURSE IN FARM COVE. BELOW: BOATING FUN

Farm Cove, The Royal Botanic Gardens, Bennelong Point, The Opera House

The Opera House, Bennelong, Government House and the Royal Botanic Gardens

The view from the Penthouse of Bennelong – No 1 Macquarie Street

ABOVE: THE VIEW FROM 'BENNELONG' OVERLOOKING THE ROYAL BOTANIC GARDENS. BELOW: THE VIEW TO THE HARBOUR BRIDGE

Bennelong
1 – 7 Macquarie Street.
Unequivocally described
as Australia's most
renowned location,
Bennelong is surrounded
by the best Sydney has to
offer, adjacent to the city
with tranquil views over
the Royal Botanic Gardens,
Sydney Opera House
and Circular Quay.

Highgate
153 Kent Street, Sydney
Positioned towards the Millers
Point end of Kent Street,
Highgate was one of the original
all-luxury high rise towers to be
completed in the northern CBD
precinct. Reminiscent of
European design, the project
comprises a high-end mix of
one, two, three and four-
bedrooms enjoying panoramic
views of Darling Harbour and
Circular Quay.

Observatory Tower
168 Kent Street, Sydney
Facing north at the foot of the
Sydney Harbour Bridge,
Observatory Tower comprises
some 193 prestige apartments
and 7 penthouse suites. Each
apartment has been meticu–
lously designed to optimise
space and maximise infinite
views across Sydney Harbour
and the Blue Mountains to
the west of Sydney.

The Pinnacle
2 Dind Street,
Milsons Point
Designed by the Rice Dabney
Group and located in the dress
circle of historic Milsons Point,
The Pinnacle offers a diverse
combination of opulent
apartments featuring spacious
internal balconies. Residents
can absorb the panoramic
harbour and city views, without
direct exposure to the elements.

The Quadrant
1 Northcliff Street,
Milsons Point
Set on the beautiful northern harbour
foreshore of Milsons Point,
The Quadrant has been designed to
provide exceptionally large apartments
with sweeping panoramic views of the
city and Sydney Harbour.
The distinct column and circular
architecture ensures maximum views
from all living areas in the apartment,
with generous balconies flowing off each
south facing room.

The public is now able to climb the famous Sydney Harbour Bridge and below right West Circular Quay (The Rocks).

harbour bridge to HOMEBUSH

Opening celebrations at Star City

Darling Harbour

Star City at Darling Harbour

Blackwattle Bay with fireworks above Darling Harbour

Above: Balmain East
Far left: Cockatoo Island
Left: Simmons Point and
Mort Bay

Above: Birchgrove with
Mort Bay across to Balmain
Right: Spectacle Island
Far right: Peacock Point
Balmain East.

Yurulbin Point, Birchgrove through to the city

Birchgrove through to Dawn Fraser Pool and White Horse Point

From the left The Iron Cove Bridge and Birkenhead Point to across the waterfronts of Drummoyne

Wrights Point, Drummoyne through to Five Dock Bay

Gladesville Bridge, Five Dock Bay to Abbottsford Bay.

Above: The old and the
new at Abbottsford Bay
Far Left: Mortlake Point
Left: Cabarita Point,
swimming pool and on to
Hen and Chicken Bay

Above: Hen and Chicken Bay and Cabarita Point
Right: Exile Bay to Canada Bay
Far right: Brays Bay Reserve to Olympic Park in the background

Rocky Point, Concord, Brays Bay to the right and Olympic Park in the background

Right:
Homebush Bay and
Mariners Cove through
to the Olympic complex
Far right:
Tarban Creek Bridge
through to Hunters Hill

Pulpitt Point

Henley

Huntley's Point

Pulpitt Point to Gladesville Bridge

St Ignatius College, Riverview between Burns Bay and Tambourine Bay on the Lane Cove River

ABOVE: NEWCOMBE POINT, HUNTERS HILL. BELOW– LEFT: BOAT SHED, MIDDLE: HUNTERS HILL, RIGHT: LUKES BAY TO PULPIT POINT, HUNTERS HILL

Alexandra Bay, Hunters Hill with the Gladesville Bridge in the background

Longueville with Woodford Bay to the front and the Lane Cove River and Hunters Hill to the rear.

Longueville to the right, Onions Point Woolwich centre, and Greenwich Point top left

southern BEACHES

South Head

Above: South Head and
the Eastern Suburbs
Near right: Dover Heights
through to the City
Far Right:Dover Heights,
North Bondi, Bondi and
Bondi Beach
Opposite: Rosa Gully,
Dover Heights

Bondi Beach

Bronte Beach, Nelson Bay to the left and Tamarama Beach to the right

Bronte baths and surf

Above top:
Shark Point, Clovelly
Above and right:
Clovelly Bay to the right,
Gordons Bay centre and
Coogee Beach to the left

South Coogee to Coogee Beach

Wylie's Baths to Coogee Beach

Mahon Pool, North Maroubra

Above top: New South Wales
Golf Course, La Perouse.
Above: St Michaels Golf Course
adjoining The Coast Golf Course.
Right: Maroubra Beach, Mahon
Pool, Mistral Point, Lurline Bay

Hungry Point, Sutherland, Gunnamatta Bay, Port Hacking and Bundenna to the top

CRONULLA PROVIDES A PEACEFUL VILLAGE ATMOSPHERE SURROUNDED BY NUMEROUS ACQUATIC ACTIVITIES

Top: Glaisher Point
Baths to Cronulla Beach
Far Right: Bass and
Flinders Point
Right: Boat Harbour

Gunamatta Bay

Gunamatta Bay, Burraneer with Burraneer Bay to the rear

Windsurfers at Brighton-Le-Sands

Our People, Our Customers, Our Future.

COLLIERS JARDINE (NSW) P/L
TONY BRASIER - CHIEF EXECUTIVE
LEVEL 26, 259 GEORGE ST, SYDNEY.
PHONE. 61 2 9257 0222
FAX. 61 2 9257 0216
www.colliersjardine.com.au

AUSTRALIAN NATIVE LANDSCAPES

Australian Native Landscapes is a privately owned company that specialises in landscape construction and the supply of a wide range of horticultural products, along with being Australia's largest recycler of organic waste materials.
The company, now in its 27th year, has been directly responsible for the landscaping of many of Sydney's landmarks, including the Chinese Gardens, First Fleet Park and Sydney's Parallel Third Runway.

ANL HEAD OFFICE
317 MONA VALE ROAD,
TERREY HILLS NSW 2084 AUSTRALIA
PHONE: (02) 9450 1444
FAX: (02) 9450 2428
email: mail@anlscape.com.au

BMW Sydney

BMW Sydney will deliver the highest standards of customer satisfaction through a team of trained, happy and committed people who have pride in the BMW Marque.

BMW SYDNEY
65 CRAIGEND STREET
RUSHCUTTERS BAY NSW 2011
PHONE: 02 9334 4555
FAX: 02 9334 4566
www.bmwsydney.com.au

ORACLE

Oracle Corporation is the world's leading supplier of software for information management, and the world's second largest independent software company. With annual revenues of over $8.3 billion, the company offers its database, tools and application products, along with related consulting, education, and support services, in more than 145 countries around the world.
In Australia and New Zealand, Oracle is one of the largest companies supplying software solutions for information management to business, industry and government. These solutions integrate database and applications technology with the Internet, World Wide Web, multi-media, video and television broadband services.

ORACLE CORPORATION AUSTRALIA PTY. LIMITED
4 JULIUS AVENUE
RIVERSIDE CORPORATE PARK
NORTH RYDE NSW 2113

WITHIN AUSTRALIA
PHONE: 1300 366 386 (WITHIN AUSTRALIA)
Email: infooracle@au.oracle.com
www.oracle.com.au

Kodak

Official Imaging
Partner of the 2000
Olympic Games

Kodak Australia has been meeting the needs of Australian photographers for over a century.

KODAK (AUSTRALIASIA) PTY LTD
LEVEL 8, 15 TALAVERA ROAD
P O BOX 10
NORTH RYDE NSW 1670
PHONE: 02 9870 4288
FAX: 02 9870 4365
Web: http://www.kodak.com.au

suburb
INDEX